Theodore Roosevelt

History
Maker
Bios

Gwenyth Swain

LERNER PUBLICATIONS COMPANY • MINNEAPOLIS

Illustrations by Tim Parlin
Map on p. 33 by Laura Westlund

Lerner Publications Company
A division of Lerner Publishing Group
241 First Avenue North
Minneapolis, MN 55401 U.S.A.

Website address: www.lernerbooks.com

Library of Congress Cataloging-in-Publication Data

Swain, Gwenyth, 1961–
    Theodore Roosevelt / by Gwenyth Swain.
      p.   cm. — (History maker bios)
    Includes bibliographical references and index.
    ISBN: 0–8225–1548–2 (lib. bdg. : alk. paper)
    1. Roosevelt, Theodore, 1858–1919—Juvenile literature. 2. Presidents—United
States—Biography—Juvenile literature. I. Title. II. Series.
E757.S98 2005
973.91'1'092—dc22   2005000553

Manufactured in the United States of America
1 2 3 4 5 6 – JR – 10 09 08 07 06 05

TABLE OF CONTENTS

INTRODUCTION

When he smiled, his teeth looked like "a row of [white ivory] dominoes." When he spoke, his words came out in high-pitched bursts, as fast as bullets from a gun. He wore thick glasses that made him look more like a professor than a politician. But wherever he went, people listened to Theodore Roosevelt, the twenty-sixth president of the United States.

He started out a sickly boy who preferred the company of animals and plants to people. But he made himself into many things: rancher, soldier, reformer, and one of the United States' most popular presidents. Whatever he did, Theodore Roosevelt was impossible *not* to notice.

This is his story.

1 TEEDIE

As a child, Theodore Roosevelt did not stand out much. He was born on October 27, 1858, in a large five-story house much like the other brownstones in his New York City neighborhood. His family was wealthy, but so were most of the other families on the block.

He was the second child born to Theodore Roosevelt and Martha Bulloch Roosevelt. Young Theodore was nicknamed Teedie, to sound like T.D. At first, Teedie was like any other little boy. But after his third birthday, he sometimes struggled to breathe. Doctors worried that he might not live long. His father spent nights pacing the floor with Teedie in his arms, gasping for air.

New York City bustled with streetcars and horse-drawn carriages when Teedie was growing up.

Asthma. That was the name the doctors gave to Teedie's sickness. In the late 1800s, doctors knew little about how to treat it. Teedie's father drove his son around the city in the cold night air. His mother took him to the Catskill Mountains in southeastern New York to get away from the city's dirty coal fires.

Young Theodore Roosevelt

What's in a Name?

Do you have a nickname? Young Theodore Roosevelt went by many names, including Teedie, Thee, and Theodore, but Teedie was his most common nickname as a boy. Later in life, he was popularly known as Teddy Roosevelt. A toy maker even created a stuffed "Teddy Bear" in his honor. But his friends never called him Teddy. He preferred the short, simple nickname TR.

Teedie never went to grade school or high school. He and his brother and two sisters studied at home, as many wealthy children did then. Theodore loved to read and was a good student. But he was a scarecrow of a boy, with bony limbs, unruly blonde hair, and blue eyes that looked off into the distance.

His father worried. When Teedie was ten years old, his father said, "Theodore, you have the mind, but you have not the body, and without the help of the body the mind cannot go as far as it should. . . . You must *make* your body." Teedie started training at a gym. Then, when his mother put weights and punching bags on an outdoor patio upstairs, he trained at home.

His chest got a little wider, but he stayed thin. He still looked off into the distance in a dreamy way—until he was fitted for a pair of glasses in 1872. Teedie was nearsighted. Glasses brought the world into focus.

Theodore Roosevelt wore glasses like these when he was young.

That summer, Theodore's father gave him a gun. Teedie had always loved studying animals near the family's summer home on Long Island. With the gun, he could shoot animals and study them up close.

When the Roosevelts went on a long vacation to Egypt, Theodore took along his glasses, his gun, and a kit for stuffing animals. He shot and studied every type of bird—kites, herons, egrets—that flew along the Nile River. Teedie loved every minute of the trip. The hot, dry Egyptian climate was good for his asthma. He wasn't sick the whole winter.

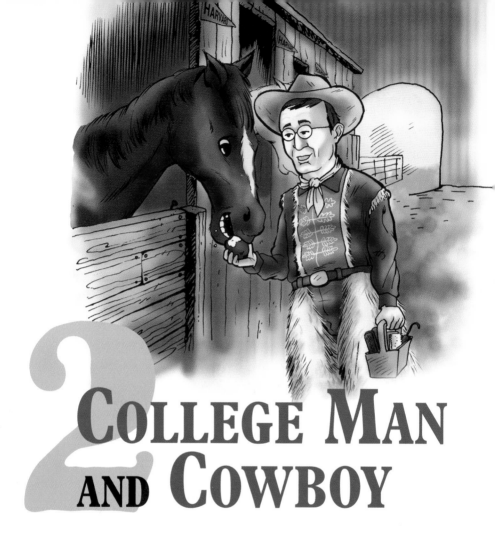

2 COLLEGE MAN AND COWBOY

Theodore stayed healthy when he finally went away to college in 1876. He went to Harvard University in Cambridge, Massachusetts. Theodore was a grown man of almost eighteen years, about five feet five inches tall and a skinny 125 pounds.

At Harvard, he didn't stand out unless he talked. His teeth were wide and white. Words seemed to burst out between them. He usually became so excited that his voice piped high and his thick glasses slid down his nose. His mother said his laugh was like an "ungreased squeak," and Teedie usually laughed a lot.

Theodore stayed at Beck Hall, his home away from home while he was at Harvard.

But Theodore didn't always find things to laugh about while at Harvard. Just after Christmas in 1878, his father died of cancer. At first, young Theodore thought he might never forget his sadness. But that fall, he met a young Boston woman named Alice Lee. Theodore quickly fell in love. Alice took some persuading. She finally agreed to marry in 1880, making Theodore happier than ever before.

Theodore met Alice Lee, his first wife, when he was a college student.

After he married and finished school, Theodore took his first steps into politics. He thought he would run for office. Maybe he would have liked to study plants and animals, as he had done at Harvard. But Theodore wanted to be noticed, and people were more likely to notice a politician than a scientist.

In fall 1881, Theodore was elected to the New York State Assembly, where state laws are made. Other assembly members thought he seemed young, eager, and overdressed. (He liked expensive, flashy clothes.)

Theodore was first elected to political office when he was twenty-three.

But people soon saw a new seriousness in Theodore Roosevelt. In 1884, shortly after giving birth to their first child, Alice Roosevelt died. Theodore's mother died the same day of typhoid fever, a dangerous and deadly disease. "The light has gone out of my life," Theodore wrote. To ease his pain, he traveled west.

The life of a cowboy appealed to Theodore.

AUTHOR! AUTHOR!

While he lived out west, Theodore Roosevelt wrote two books, *Ranch Life and the Hunting Trail* and *Hunting Trips of a Ranchman.* Over the years, he wrote dozens of other books. A collection of the letters he wrote to his children (complete with sketches he drew) became a best-seller after his death.

He bought a ranch in the Badlands of the Dakota Territory. (This land later became part of South Dakota.) There, he rode horses, rounded up cattle with cowboys, and wrote stories about the West. When he was ready to return to politics, Theodore was fit and tan and free of asthma. He was ready to make a mark.

3A ROUGH RIDE

The first impression Theodore
Roosevelt made when he returned to
politics was as a loser. Theodore entered
the race for mayor of New York in 1886 as
the "Cowboy Candidate." He lost badly.

After marrying a childhood friend named Edith Carow, he took a series of government jobs. He worked in Washington, D.C., and was a police commissioner, or person in charge of police, in New York City. He was named assistant secretary of the navy by President William McKinley. But he didn't give up on politics.

Edith Carow was Theodore's second wife.

Before Theodore could run for office again, the United States was facing war. In Cuba, people protested against the Spanish, who ruled the island south of Florida. Worried about the protests, the United States sent warships to the area. In February 1898, the battleship USS *Maine* blew up in Cuba's Havana Harbor. The U.S. government believed Spain was to blame. By April, the United States was at war with Spain.

When Theodore headed off to Cuba with the Rough Riders, he carried twelve pairs of glasses. He wanted to be sure he always had one at hand.

A GOOD STORY

Theodore Roosevelt was an eager reader. He knew how a good newspaper story could make readers notice a person. Over the years, Theodore learned how to *be* a good story. He was always ready to answer reporters' questions. He was happy to pose for photographs. His smile and clothes were eye-catching. As a Rough Rider, he wore a bright bandana and broad-brimmed hat. They made him seem less like a wealthy gentleman and more like an everyday hero.

Theodore Roosevelt soon quit his job and organized a volunteer regiment, or large group, of the army. The regiment was made up of cowboys, New York policemen, and friends from Harvard. All were part of Roosevelt's "Rough Riders." They fought their biggest battle in July 1898.

COL. ROOSEVELT

Tells the story of

THE ROUGH RIDERS

in Scribner's Magazine. It begins in January and will run for six months, with many illustrations from photographs taken in the field.

JANUARY SCRIBNER'S
NOW READY PRICE 25 CENTS

Theodore wrote about his experiences with the Rough Riders.

Americans hoped to capture Spanish ships in the Cuban city of Santiago. While U.S. Navy ships waited nearby, army troops landed fifteen miles away. Under Theodore's leadership, the Rough Riders charged up Kettle Hill and helped capture San Juan Hill. Taking over the hill let Americans eventually capture the city of Santiago. One out of three Rough Riders died, but Roosevelt lived. "I never expected to come through!" he wrote home. "I am as strong as a bull moose."

When Theodore ran for governor of New York State that November, he was a winner. At forty, he was the youngest person elected to the job. He and Edith and their family—Alice, Theodore Jr., Kermit, Ethel, Archibald, and Quentin—settled into the governor's mansion in Albany, New York.

Theodore and Edith Roosevelt sit for a family portrait. The Roosevelts pose at Sagamore Hill, the family home on Long Island, New York.

"All together," Roosevelt wrote to a friend, "I am pretty well satisfied with what I have accomplished." He brought inspectors into factories, making sure that people worked in safe conditions. He stopped sawmills from dumping waste into mountain rivers and streams. And he raised pay for teachers.

When he considered other jobs, he thought he might run for president. But in 1899, Vice President Garret A. Hobart died. Suddenly, everyone was talking about *Vice President* Theodore Roosevelt.

Theodore Roosevelt helped many people in New York during his term as governor.

Theodore Roosevelt and William McKinley were running mates in 1900.

Theodore didn't want the job, even though President McKinley was a friend. "The vice president . . . ," he wrote, "is really a fifth wheel to the coach. It is not a stepping stone to anything but oblivion [being forgotten]." Even worse, the job didn't pay well. Edith worried that the family would have to scrimp and save if Theodore became vice president.

No one listened to Roosevelt's protests. In 1900, he finally agreed to run and was elected vice president of the United States.

President McKinley (THIRD FROM RIGHT) was shot by Leon Czolgosz (CENTER WITH CLOTH AROUND HAND). McKinley died eight days later.

Both the president and vice president traveled to meet the public. On September 6, 1901, Roosevelt was in Vermont. McKinley was in Buffalo, New York. The president spent hours shaking hands. One man, named Leon Czolgosz, seemed to have an injured hand. It was wrapped in a cloth. He held out his other hand toward McKinley, but the two never shook. Instead, Czolgosz shot McKinley with a revolver hidden under the cloth.

At first, President McKinley seemed likely to recover. The danger appeared to have passed. But on September 14, 1901, McKinley died. At age forty-two, Theodore Roosevelt became the youngest person to serve as president of the United States.

Roosevelt went right on being a father and playmate. And he put a lot of energy toward being president. (He got some of that energy from drinking coffee in a large cup Ted Jr. said was "more in the nature of a bathtub.")

Roosevelt's ideas fit in with the Progressive movement of the early 1900s. Some Progressives were Republicans, like Theodore Roosevelt. Others were Democrats. All wanted change. They wanted laws to control big business, such as railroads and meat-packing plants. They wanted laws to protect buyers. They demanded the breakup of huge trusts. These groups of big businesses worked together to raise profits, shut down small companies, and pay workers low wages.

As a Progressive, Roosevelt joined with reformers such as Jane Addams (RIGHT) to help old people, poor people, and children.

President Roosevelt thought that the Northern Securities Company needed to be stopped. It controlled railroads in the Northwest. Northern Securities charged farmers high prices to send crops to market. Northern Securities owned so many railroads no other company could compete.

In the 1900s, trains were almost the only way to carry crops from the countryside into the city to be sold.

President Roosevelt, SECOND FROM LEFT, *meeting with coal mine owners and workers*

Roosevelt asked the U.S. goverment to file a lawsuit against Northern Securities in 1902. The lawsuit lasted two years. Finally the Supreme Court agreed with the president. In the eyes of the public, Theodore Roosevelt was becoming a "trustbuster."

In the summer of 1902, coal miners in eastern Pennsylvania were on strike. They wanted better pay. Mine owners refused. Roosevelt knew that if the strike lasted into winter, many Americans would not be able to get coal to heat their homes. Many would be cold. Some might even die.

The president invited miners and mine owners to meet with him. He convinced them to keep the mines open—keeping Americans warm that winter. Later, Roosevelt said he'd meant to be fair and give the miners and the owners "a square deal." Before long, that was the name given to Roosevelt's ideas as president.

Not everyone agreed that Roosevelt offered a "square deal." Roosevelt wanted to build a canal across Central America. The best route cut through Panama. It was then owned by Colombia, a country in South America. But the United States and Colombia could not agree on a fair deal for the land.

The Panama Canal greatly shortened the distance a ship had to travel to get from New York City to San Francisco.

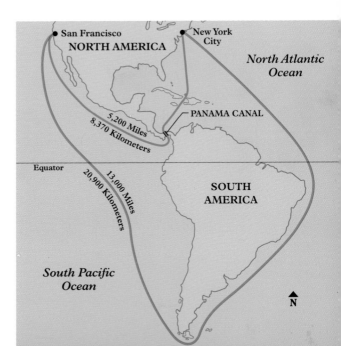

In November 1903, Panama rose up against Colombia and formed the Republic of Panama. The U.S. government immediately recognized the new republic. The United States signed a deal paying Panama, not Colombia, for land for the canal. Colombians felt cheated, but in 1904, the United States began building the canal anyway. The canal was finished in 1914. Roosevelt considered it one of his top accomplishments as president.

It took ten years to complete work on the Panama Canal.

THE BIG STICK

"I have always been fond of the West African proverb," Roosevelt wrote, "'Speak softly and carry a big stick; you will go far.'" As president, Roosevelt tried to live by this saying. He sent U.S. Navy ships around the world, making a show of power (the big stick). But he often used meetings (speaking softly) to end conflicts, such as the Russian-Japanese War.

Also high on that list was Roosevelt's attempt to end war between Japan and Russia. Roosevelt urged both sides to sit down and talk in Portsmouth, New Hampshire. He followed the talks from his summer home, Sagamore Hill, on Long Island. When it seemed that Russia and Japan would never agree, Roosevelt managed to keep the two sides talking.

Both countries signed a treaty, or agreement, in September 1905. For his work, Roosevelt was awarded the Nobel Peace Prize in 1906. He was the first American honored with this major prize.

Before Theodore Roosevelt, most presidents had approved or disapproved laws passed by Congress. Roosevelt pushed through laws of his own. He argued for the Meat Inspection Act. It sent government inspectors into meat-packing plants. He fought for the Pure Food and Drug Act and the Hepburn Act, which set rules for railroads.

Roosevelt (CENTER) helped Japan's minister (LEFT) and Russia's minister (RIGHT) resolve the dispute between their countries.

Although he was popular, Theodore Roosevelt did not run for reelection in 1908. Roosevelt worried that a president might become too much like like a king if he governed for too many years.

He would miss the spotlight. But more than anything, he felt lucky. "I realize to the full," he wrote to one of his sons, "how very lucky I have been, not only to be President but to have been able to accomplish so much while President."

5 THE GOOD FIGHT

Roosevelt was fifty but still ready for adventures. With his son Kermit, he set off for Africa. He shot lions, zebras, hippos, and other animals. Most were stuffed and displayed at U.S. museums.

Roosevelt traveled to Africa with his son Kermit.

Roosevelt wrote about his hunts in magazine articles that were published as a book called *African Game Trails*. The U.S. newspapers were full of stories of his latest catches in Africa.

When he returned to the United States in 1910, Roosevelt was as popular as ever. The man in the White House, President William Howard Taft, was not. Roosevelt had backed Taft, a Republican, when he ran for president in 1908. Roosevelt had hoped Taft would continue Progressive ideas.

But Taft was a disappointment to Roosevelt and to Progressives across the country. In 1912, Roosevelt hoped the Republican Party would pick him to run for president. But the party picked Taft. Roosevelt didn't accept defeat. Instead, he joined other Progressives to form a third party that some called the Bull Moose Party. He fought against the Republican Taft and the Democrat Woodrow Wilson, who were running for president.

Roosevelt's supporters gather at a Bull Moose convention.

THE BULL MOOSE

In 1912, Progressives swayed Roosevelt to run for president. They called their party the Progressive Party, but newspapers and the public were soon calling it the Bull Moose Party. (Roosevelt was fond of saying he was as strong as a moose.) "If you wish me to make the fight," Roosevelt told Progressives, "I will make it, even if only one state should support me!" The Bull Moose Party won five states but lost the three-way race.

The campaign was short but almost deadly. While waving to crowds in Milwaukee, Wisconsin, Roosevelt was shot in the chest. The shooter, John F. Schrank, was mentally ill. Roosevelt was saved by his metal eyeglasses case and campaign speech. Both were in his breast pocket and partly blocked the bullets.

Roosevelt couldn't read his speech. The bullet had passed through all fifty folded pages. But he spoke as planned before a large audience. After talking for an hour and a half, he was finally treated for his wounds. Americans were impressed by his bravery, but not enough voted for him as president. Wilson won the election. "We have fought the good fight," Roosevelt wrote to a friend, "we have kept the faith, and we have nothing to regret."

Theodore Roosevelt, age fifty-seven

Roosevelt's house, Sagamore Hill, on Long Island

Those words echoed through the last years of his life. Roosevelt wrote the story of his life, traveled down a river in South America, and urged the United States to enter World War I. His sons fought in that war. His youngest, Quentin, was killed in 1918 while flying behind enemy lines. But Roosevelt's own fighting days were over. Illness forced him to bed at Sagamore Hill. He died there in his sleep on January 6, 1919.

Everyone noticed. The nation mourned.

TIMELINE

THEODORE ROOSEVELT WAS
BORN ON OCTOBER 27,
1858.

In the year . . .

1861   Theodore began to suffer from childhood asthma.   Age 3

1872   in the summer, he got eyeglasses.
his father gave him a gun.

1876   he went to school for the first time, to Harvard.   Age 18

1880   he graduated from Harvard.
he married Alice Lee.

1884   Alice gave birth to a girl, also named Alice, and died days later.

1885   he went on a spring cattle roundup in the Dakota Badlands.   Age 27

1886   he married Edith Carow, a childhood friend.

1898   he led the Rough Riders in the Spanish-American War in Cuba.   Age 39
he was elected governor of New York.   Age 40

1901   he served as vice president under William McKinley, who was killed in September.
he became the twenty-sixth president of the United States.   Age 42

1904   work began on the Panama Canal.   Age 45
Theodore was elected president.

1906   he signed the Hepburn Act, Pure Food and Drug Act, and Meat Inspection Act.

1912   he ran unsuccessfully for president as the Bull Moose (Progressive) candidate.   Age 54

1919   he died at Sagamore Hill on January 6.   Age 60

LEGACY IN LAND

If you want to see what Theodore Roosevelt accomplished as president, look at the nation's parkland. Roosevelt protected forty million acres of national forests. He carved out five national parks and fifty-one national wildlife refuges. He created sixteen national monuments, including Niagara Falls and the Grand Canyon. Roosevelt was driven by his love of nature.

Roosevelt preserved so much land, some worried he was going too far. One writer was partly serious when he warned that if Roosevelt wasn't stopped, "there would be little ground left to bury folks on."

When Roosevelt saw the Grand Canyon in 1903, he called it "wonderful and beautiful beyond descripton."

Further Reading

NONFICTION

Fritz, Jean. *Bully for You, Teddy Roosevelt!* New York: G. P. Putnam's, 1991. An entertaining look at Roosevelt's life for readers ages 10 to 14.

Harness, Cheryl. *Young Teddy Roosevelt.* Washington, D.C.: National Geographic Society, 1998. A picture-book biography focusing on the years before Roosevelt's presidency.

Roosevelt, Theodore. *The Boyhood Diary of Theodore Roosevelt, 1869–1870: Early Travels of the 26th U.S. President.* Edited by Shelley Swanson Sateren. Mankato, MN: Blue Earth Books, 2001. Introduces young readers to Roosevelt through selections from his diaries.

FICTION

Hines, Gary. *A Christmas Tree in the White House.* New York: Henry Holt, 1998. When President Roosevelt refuses to cut down a pine tree for Christmas, his youngest sons take matters into their own hands.

Monjo, F. N. *The One Bad Thing about Father.* New York: Harper & Row, 1970. In this book for beginning readers, one of Roosevelt's sons describes life at the White House.

WEBSITES

The Theodore Roosevelt Association
<http://www.theodoreroosevelt.org> This wide-ranging
website explores Roosevelt's legacy.

Theodore Roosevelt Birthplace National Historic Site
<http://www.nps.gov/thrb/> This website describes
Roosevelt's New York City birthplace, which is open to the
public.

SELECT BIBLIOGRAPHY

Dalton, Kathleen. *Theodore Roosevelt: A Strenuous Life.*
New York: Alfred A. Knopf, 2002.

McCullough, David. *Mornings on Horseback.* New York:
Simon & Schuster, 1981.

Miller, Nathan. *Theodore Roosevelt: A Life.* New York:
William Morrow and Company, Inc., 1992.

Morris, Edmund. *Theodore Rex.* New York: Random House,
2001.

Morris, Edmund. *The Rise of Theodore Roosevelt.* New
York: The Modern Library, 2001.

Roosevelt, Theodore. *Theodore Roosevelt, An
Autobiography.* 1913. Reprint, New York: Da Capo Press,
1985.

Roosevelt, Theodore. *Theodore Roosevelt's Letters to His
Children.* Edited by Joseph Bucklin Bishop. New York:
Charles Scribner's Sons, 1919.

INDEX

Acknowledgments

For photographs and artwork: © Hulton|Archive by Getty Images, pp. 4, 31; Library of Congress, pp. 7, 14, 16, 19, 20, 22, 25, 26, 29, 34, 40, 42, 43; Theodore Roosevelt Collection, Harvard College Library, p. 8, 23; Image by Will Dunniway, p. 10; © Bettmann/CORBIS, p. 13; © Brown Brothers, pp. 15, 24, 39; The Boston Journal, p. 30; HistoryPictures.com, p. 32; © North Wind Picture Archive, p. 36; © A.A.M. Van Der Heyden/Independent Picture Service, p. 45. Front cover: Library of Congress. Back cover: © Jim Simondent/Independent Picture Service.

For quoted material: pp. 5, 22, 24, 25, 30, 32, 33, 35, 41, 42, 45 (text), Miller, Nathan, *Theodore Roosevelt: A Life* (New York: William Morrow and Company, Inc., 1992); pp. 10, 13, 16, McCullough, David, *Mornings on Horseback* (New York: Simon & Schuster, 1981); pp. 29 (both), 37, 45 (caption); Roosevelt, Theodore, *Theodore Roosevelt's Letters to His Children,* edited by Joseph Bucklin Bishop (New York: Charles Scribner's Sons, 1919).

LITTLE DEE
AND THE PENGUIN
THE

by Christopher Baldwin

Dial Books for Young Readers

For Miles and Arlo

DIAL BOOKS FOR YOUNG READERS
PENGUIN YOUNG READERS GROUP
An imprint of Penguin Random House, LLC
375 Hudson Street
New York, NY 10014

Library of Congress Cataloging-in-Publication Data

Baldwin, Christopher, date.
Little Dee and the penguin / by Christopher Baldwin.
pages   cm
Summary: After her park ranger father dies, Little Dee is swept off on an adventure with a group of animals as they try to protect their penguin friend from being eaten by a pair of hungry polar bears.
1. Graphic novels. [1. Graphic novels. 2. Human-animal relationships—Fiction. 3. Animals—Fiction. 4. Humorous stories.] I. Title.
PZ7.7.B28Li 2016   741.5'973—dc23   2015010378

Printed in China
PB ISBN 978-0-8037-4108-9
Library Binding ISBN 978-1-101-99429-0

1 3 5 7 9 10 8 6 4 2

Book design by Jasmin Rubero
Text hand-lettered by Christopher Baldwin